How to Be a Samurai Warrior

Written by
Fiona Macdonald

Illustrated by
John James

NATIONAL GEOGRAPHIC
Washington, D.C.

First published in North America in 2005 by
NATIONAL GEOGRAPHIC SOCIETY
1145 17th Street, N.W.
Washington, D.C. 20036-4688

Trade ISBN: 0-7922-3618-1
Library ISBN: 0-7922-3633-5

Library of Congress Cataloging-in-Publication Data available on request.

Printed in China

Series created and designed by David Salariya
Penny Clarke, Editor

For the National Geographic Society
Bea Jackson, Art Director
Virginia Ann Koeth, Project Editor

Dr. John Weste, Fact Consultant
Tutor in medieval and modern Japanese history at the University of Durham

Photographic credits
t=top b=bottom c=center l=left r=right

The Art Archive: 7
The Art Archive / Gunshots: 11, 27r
The Art Archive / Eileen Tweedy: 29
The Art Archive / Museo Stibbert Florence / Dagli Orti: 9
The Art Archive / Oriental Art Museum Genoa / Dagli Orti(A):
12, 15, 27l

The Art Archive / V & A Museum London/ Sally Chappell: 20

Every effort has been made to trace copyright holders.
The Salariya Book Company apologizes for any unintentional
omissions and would be pleased, in such cases, to add an
acknowledgment in future editions.

One of the world's largest nonprofit scientific and educational organizations, the National Geographic Society was founded in 1888 "for the increase and diffusion of geographic knowledge." Fulfilling this mission, the Society educates and inspires millions every day through its magazines, books, television programs, videos, maps and atlases, research grants, the National Geographic Bee, teacher workshops, and innovative classroom materials. The Society is supported through membership dues, charitable gifts, and income from the sale of its educational products. This support is vital to National Geographic's mission to increase global understanding and promote conservation of our planet through exploration, research, and education.

For more information, please call 1-800-NGS LINE (647-5463) or write to the following address:
National Geographic Society
1145 17th Street N.W.
Washington, D.C. 20036-4688 U.S.A.
Visit the Society's Web site at www.nationalgeographic.com.

Samurai Needed

How would you like to join a fearsome fighting force and serve as a samurai?

Samurai are elite Japanese warriors—self-disciplined, honorable, and brave. They fight in private armies, led by daimyo (local lords). Daimyo and samurai are very powerful. They fight against other daimyo and samurai and, sometimes, the shogun—the mighty army commander and real ruler of Japan.

Your main duties will include:

• leaving your home to fight if your daimyo summons you

• following "the way of the warrior"—rules for samurai behavior

• studying ancient wisdom, writing poetry, and admiring art

(An interest in Japan and Japanese civilization would be a great advantage.)

Apply in writing to your local daimyo or to the shogun's court.

Contents

What You Should Know

This is a journey in time and place: back about 400 years to the Land of the Rising Sun—the homeland of the samurai. Foreigners call it Japan.

Japan has hundreds of islands. Earthquakes and active volcanoes are common. Each local area belongs to a daimyo. For centuries they have led samurai to fight in bloody civil wars. But now, Japan is changing. A few years ago, in 1603, daimyo Tokugawa Ieyasu (1542–1616) defeated all the other warring lords. He became shogun and built a new capital city, Edo. He's ordered many samurai to live there.

Japan

HOKKAIDO

Hirosaki Castle

SEA OF JAPAN

Bitchu-Matsuyama Castle

HONSHU

Kyoto

Edo/ Tokyo

Osaka

SHIKOKU

KYUSHU

Kōchi Castle

Matsuyama Castle

To make sure he stayed in control, he banished many samurai families to outlaying lands (*shown in red*).

5

Are You from a Samurai Family?

To be a real samurai you have to come from the right family. Were your male ancestors samurai? Does your family own land and control peasant farmers? You answered "yes"? You qualify. If you're not from a samurai family, don't give up hope. You can try to claim samurai status by showing exceptional loyalty, bravery, and fighting skill.

▶ You must be born a boy. All samurai are men.

Help from your father

▼ Learn from your father. He will teach you to be polite, obedient, and self-controlled. He will encourage you to honor your ancestors and to be proud of your family.

A girl's future

▲ If you're born a girl, you can't be a true samurai. Your task will be to serve your father—and, later, your husband and sons. Your parents will choose your husband from another samurai family. They'll base their choice on his high rank or political connections. You cannot refuse to marry him.

◀ If you're a girl from a low-ranking family you'll work as a servant in a samurai home.

▶ This porcelain statue of a woman wearing a long, loose kimono was made around A.D. 1600. When he is relaxing a samurai also wears a kimono.

▼ Kendo, judo, and karate improve women's fitness and strength.

The role of a wife

▲ As a wife you must bear a son who will inherit your husband's land. You must also offer your husband wise advice. If you have daughters, teach them elegant, modest manners, how to run a home, and how to read and write. For self-defense and fitness, they can learn martial arts.

What Will You Learn?

You've heard older warriors say, "Samurai are born, not made." Let's hope you have inherited samurai qualities, such as strength and speed, from your family. They'll be useful on the battlefield. But long before you're ready to fight, you must devote yourself to study. You must submit to harsh lessons from school-teachers and sword-masters. They will train your body and discipline your mind. It takes many years to learn to be a samurai. So don't give up or feel discouraged.

▼ You can't be left-handed. Samurai hold swords in the right hand, especially when fighting side by side. Your teacher will tie back your left hand, forcing you to use your right. This may feel very strange. But with practice, your right hand will become strong enough for fighting.

Going to school

School starts when you are about ▶ seven years old. You'll learn reading and writing, martial arts, stories about samurai heroes, and games of strategy, such as Go.

Learning to fight

▲ A sword-master will teach you how to fight. At first you'll use wooden sticks. These will train you to be quick and agile, so that you can defend yourself. Your classmates will watch your lessons. Don't disgrace yourself by showing weakness or fear.

▲ When you leave school, you'll be given a new hairstyle and armor. The armor below, made of wicker (woven twigs) and metal, dates from about 1700.

Becoming a man

When you're between 12 and 18 you'll take part in a *genbuku* ceremony, to show you're an adult. You'll say good-bye to your mother and choose a new name. Soon after, you'll start samurai duties, guarding your lord's land.

Can You Use Deadly Weapons?

How many weapons can you handle? Traditionally, samurai fight with bows and arrows, daggers, swords, and spears. Swords are the samurai's special weapon. You'll always carry two—a long curved *tachi* or a *katana*, and a shorter, broader *wakizashi* blade. Your father has taught you this old saying: "A samurai always sleeps with his sword by his side."

Deadly weapons

▼ Japanese swordsmiths are the best in the world. Before starting work, they pray and bathe. They heat, roll, and fold steel strips thousands of times to make strong, springy blades, then grind them to razor sharpness.

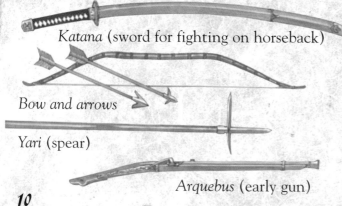

Tachi (sword for fighting on foot)

Katana (sword for fighting on horseback)

Bow and arrows

Yari (spear)

Arquebus (early gun)

▼ It's very difficult to shoot arrows while galloping on horseback. Samurai practice by shooting at dogs.

These special arrows shriek as they fly through the air.

The effect of guns

◄ The first guns reached Japan from Europe in 1542. They could kill from 220 yards (about 200 m) away—keeping gunmen safely out of reach of all traditional weapons. Although samurai still use swords, spears, and bows and arrows, guns are changing the way they fight battles.

Hand-to-hand fighting with swords

▲ You'll need many different battle skills. Can you slash with your sword, stab with your dagger, and thrust with your spear? Can you fight on foot, wrestle enemies, gallop on horseback, and capture prisoners?

Tanto (dagger)

They're old-fashioned, but they still terrify enemies.

Traditional battles

Before guns arrived, many battles were fought like duels. Samurai lined up face-to-face and challenged each other to individual swordfights. Now commanders order whole armies to shoot at each other with guns, then to charge at each other with spears.

▲ A *tanto* (very sharp dagger) and its sheath. Daggers kill at close quarters. The finest Japanese weapons are given names. Some samurai say weapons have magic powers.

11

Can You Afford Armor?

Before 1450, your ancestors protected themselves with boxlike tunics of sheet metal. But you prefer lighter, close-fitting armor made of metal strips laced together or carefully shaped steel plates. Can't afford this? Then try small metal squares fixed to a shirt of chain mail.

Frightening enemies

▶ Add a metal "devil-face" mask to your helmet to frighten enemies. If you like, you can add fierce beards and moustaches made of thick horsehair.

▼ Paint your metal face mask red. It's the sign of anger.

◀ Skilled craftworkers make and mend your armor.

▶ *Tsuba* (sword hilts) protect the hand holding the sword.

Head protection

▼ Your helmet has up to 32 curved metal panels riveted together and a neck guard of metal strips. Daimyos' helmets have crests of painted wood.

◄ For comfort, wear a loincloth, short kimono, baggy pants, and a padded cap under your armor.

► Your armor is held in place by strong leather strips tied at the back and is decorated with silk cords.

Lice!

► Be warned! Most armor is very heavy—a suit can weigh 40 pounds (18 kg). It is also hot and uncomfortable to wear. It traps sweat and is a breeding ground for lice. After a battle, hang your armor over a smoky fire to get rid of the bugs, germs, and smells.

Helmet with crest

Sword

Neck guard

Shoulder guard

Hand armor

Breastplate

Armored kilt

Knee protectors

Shin guard

Straw sandals

Do You Have the Right Attitude

To be a successful samurai your mind must be as strong as your body. Learn to control your thoughts and feelings. Be calm. Think carefully. Most important of all, follow Bushido—the strict code of behavior that has guided samurai for centuries. Bushido demands bravery, discipline, loyalty, honor, honesty, and obedience. It will teach you that is better to die bravely than to live in disgrace.

Practicing meditation

▼ Find time each day for Zen meditation in a quiet room or peaceful garden. The stillness will help clear your mind.

Religion

What are your beliefs? Do you pray at a Buddhist temple? Or do you follow Shinto, the ancient Japanese faith, and make offerings to *kami* (nature spirits)? Perhaps, like many samurai, you admire the teachings of both religions.

Zen

◄ Some samurai follow the Zen branch of the Buddhist faith. This was brought to Japan soon after A.D. 1100 by two Buddhist monks, Eisai and Dogen. Their followers learn to meditate. They hope this will lead to enlightenment.

14

The Buddha

▼ The Buddha (enlightened one) was a wise Indian prince who lived and taught around 500 B.C. Japanese artists portray him in many forms. Often he is shown as Kannon, god of mercy.

▲ Shoguns such as Minamoto Yoritomo (above) commanded complete loyalty as part of the Bushido code.

Teachers and pupils

▲ Make time to study ancient wisdom passed down by monks, poets, and philosophers. It will help strengthen your mind. You'll find teachers living in the peaceful countryside.

Wooden statue of the Buddha/ Kannon, made in Japan between A.D. 1350 and 1550

15

Will You Be Loyal?

The word "samurai" means "someone who serves." Samurai must honor the emperor, respect the shogun, and offer loyal, obedient service to their daimyo. There are three ranks of samurai. Daimyo, at the top, serve as army commanders. Next are *hatamoto* (officers) and then *go-kenin* (loyal followers). A samurai's rank depends on how much land his family owns. If he captures land in battle he may be promoted.

Supplying soldiers

Samurai have to supply troops to fight in their daimyo's army. The number depends on how much rice is produced on a samurai's land. This is measured in *koku*—the amount of rice that feeds one man for a year. For each 100 koku, a samurai might have to supply six soldiers and equip them with weapons.

Archer

Arquebusier

Ashigaru (ordinary soldiers) come from low-ranking families. They fight alongside samurai but are rarely promoted to samurai rank.

▼ Ashigaru carry *nobori*, long, narrow flags with their daimyo's crest. It's an honor but makes them easy targets for enemies.

Ashigaru (ordinary soldiers)

Daimyo (samurai lord)

Daimyo

Shogun (supreme commander)

▲ The shogun rules on behalf of the emperor. "Shogun" means "supreme general who conquers barbarians." In the past, the shoguns came from different families, such as the Minamoto and the Ashikaga, who took power because they were talented leaders and good at war. But since 1603 all shoguns have come from the Tokugawa family. Daimyo are the richest, most powerful samurai. They own vast estates and fine castles and lead armies of thousands of men.

Flag-bearer

Army commander

Spearman

Foot soldier

Bodyguard

Could You Survive on Campaign

Each year, you'll spend weeks or months away from home on patrol. You'll need to defend your lord's land—and your own—against attacking enemies. You might be ordered to advance through hostile territory to make war on a rival lord or even to fight in the shogun's army against invading foreigners. Japan's wild, rugged landscape means that ambush is a constant danger. Enemy samurai may be waiting in mountain valleys or thick forests, ready to attack.

▼ When on patrol or campaign in dangerous lands, you might need to rely on the knowledge you've learned from books. *The Art of War*, written in the 5th century B.C., advises: "Birds rising in flight ahead is a sign that the enemy are waiting to ambush you."

Watch the left side!

Food on campaign

You'll have to carry all you need with you, including food. For a quick, simple meal, try cooked dried rice. Just mix it with water (boiled in your helmet), then add dried tuna for flavor. Or go hunting for rabbit and deer.

Finding shelter

◀ On campaign, you shelter in temples or huddle under bushes or in barns. Your commander might pitch a *tobari* (circle of tents and flags) or build a temporary wooden fort.

Getting dressed for battle

(1) Put on a loincloth.
(2) Add a short kimono.
(3) Tie baggy trousers around waist.
(4) Fasten shin guards.

(5) Fix thigh guards.
(6) Pull on chain mail.
(7) Add chest guard.
(8) Buckle on body armor (tie with silk cord).

(9) Cover hair with cloth scarf.
(10) Tie on helmet; arrange shoulder guards and face mask.

Extra dangers

Take care in camp at night and be wary of ninja fighters. The ninjas study special martial arts to move silently and quickly so you will not notice them. They might sneak in at night and steal your battle plans or kill your lord.

People in the army

You'll meet all sorts of people in the army. Everyone has a special job to do. There are cooks, baggage-handlers, grooms (who look after the horses), pages, flag-carriers, porters (to carry spare weapons), builders, body-guards, spies, and signalers (who send secret messages with gongs and drums). There are also army doctors, but they only care for senior samurai. Ordinary soldiers rely on traditional remedies, such as bathing wounds in heated urine to ease pain.

Will You Live in a Castle?

Y ou're living when Japan's greatest castles are being built. Like earlier castles, they guard important sites, such as river-crossings or mountain passes. They have stone foundations and are surrounded by moats, ramparts, and walls. But the new castles are much bigger and very beautiful. Most have many towers and are several stories high. They have painted plaster walls, carved woodwork, and steep, soaring roofs. Inside, they are elegant and comfortable. They are status symbols, proclaiming their owner's wealth and power.

Magnificently decorated storage chest from about A.D. 1650.

Kitchens, stables, workshops, lavatories for soldiers

Inner walls

Outer walls

Moat

The role of castles

Castles are built for defense, but they are also homes for daimyo and samurai families and offices for managing lands and farms. Many people work in the castles—builders, decorators, cleaners, cooks, housemaids, stable-hands, gardeners, administrators, and scribes. Servants recruited from nearby farms work in the castle. Their lives are hard, and they must always show respect to the owner of the castle and his family.

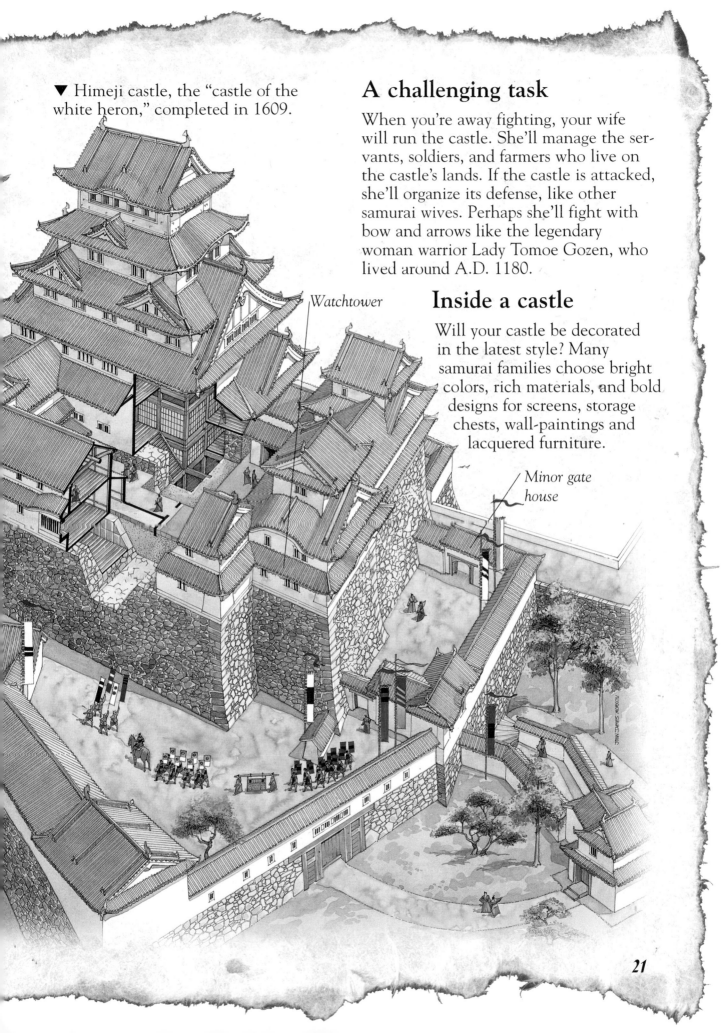

▼ Himeji castle, the "castle of the white heron," completed in 1609.

A challenging task

When you're away fighting, your wife will run the castle. She'll manage the servants, soldiers, and farmers who live on the castle's lands. If the castle is attacked, she'll organize its defense, like other samurai wives. Perhaps she'll fight with bow and arrows like the legendary woman warrior Lady Tomoe Gozen, who lived around A.D. 1180.

Inside a castle

Will your castle be decorated in the latest style? Many samurai families choose bright colors, rich materials, and bold designs for screens, storage chests, wall-paintings and lacquered furniture.

Watchtower

Minor gate house

Will You Be Part of a Siege?

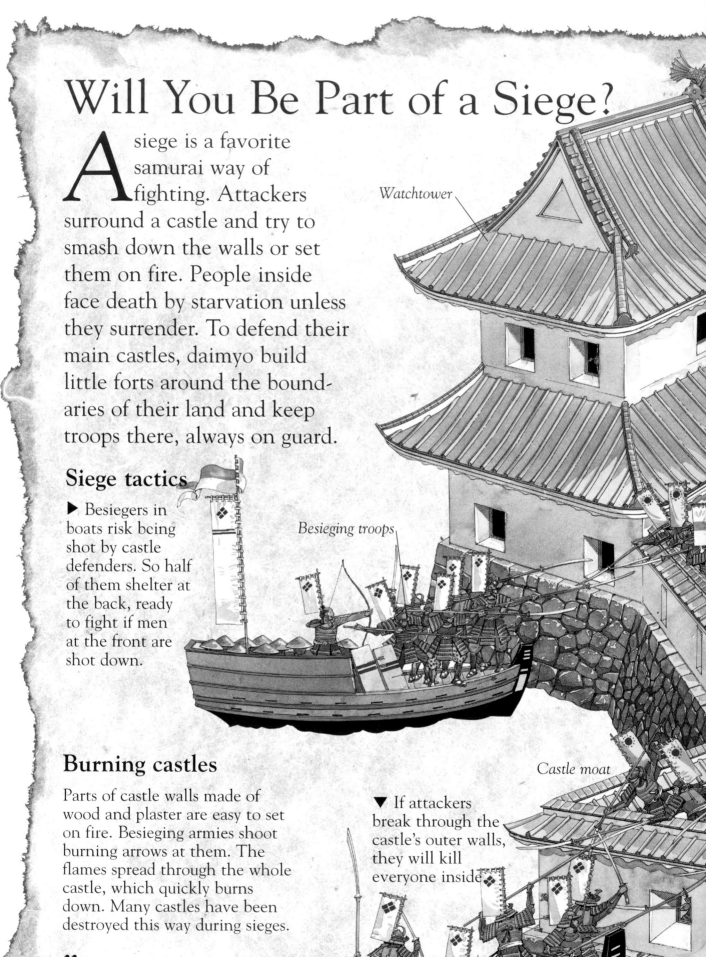

A siege is a favorite samurai way of fighting. Attackers surround a castle and try to smash down the walls or set them on fire. People inside face death by starvation unless they surrender. To defend their main castles, daimyo build little forts around the boundaries of their land and keep troops there, always on guard.

Siege tactics

▶ Besiegers in boats risk being shot by castle defenders. So half of them shelter at the back, ready to fight if men at the front are shot down.

Watchtower

Besieging troops

Castle moat

Burning castles

Parts of castle walls made of wood and plaster are easy to set on fire. Besieging armies shoot burning arrows at them. The flames spread through the whole castle, which quickly burns down. Many castles have been destroyed this way during sieges.

▼ If attackers break through the castle's outer walls, they will kill everyone inside.

A wife's help

Hosokawa Jako (1542–1616) helped defend her husband's castle. She climbed up to the roof and spied on enemy soldiers far below. Then she drew a plan of their camp with her make-up—so that her husband's soldiers knew where to attack.

Castle yard

▲ Defenders fire from the castle's small, deep windows, so it's difficult for the attackers to see them.

Would You Visit a Town?

You've seen farmers' markets and ports beside the sea, but have you been to a new castle town? They're springing up all over Japan. Samurai can live next to their daimyo's castle—but low-ranking people have to stay a respectful distance away. Towns are the ideal place for them. A whole new way of life is developing in towns based on business, money, and pleasure—quite unlike the traditional samurai lifestyle.

▶ Japan has many natural hot springs. They're just the place for samurai to relax and refresh themselves after hard fighting.

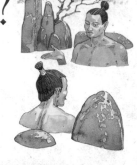

Lowly but essential

▼ Town traders and craftworkers are low ranking, compared with samurai. But they sell essential food and drink, and make all kinds of useful goods.

New ways of living

▲ New castle towns are well planned, with walls, streets, gates, bridges, watchtowers, and freshwater. There are separate living zones for soldiers, workers, traders and their families, and entertainers. Off-duty samurai visit towns to relax and enjoy themselves.

▼ Kite flying is a popular sport at festivals. Samurai use kites for signaling in wartime.

Girl   *Joyful old man*   *Kind old man*

Angry woman   *Jealous woman*   *Warrior*

Masks for Noh plays

▲ Traditional Noh plays are popular with samurai. Noh actors wear masks to show the characters they are playing. The masks' spirits are said to inspire them.

Theater for performing Noh plays

Noh theater

◀ Noh plays are very ancient and have religious origins. The actors are all men. Like samurai, they are well-trained, disciplined, and powerful.

Do You Want the Top Job?

According to law and tradition, the emperor is top man in Japan. He's honored like a god and claims descent from the sun-goddess. So you could never hope to get his job. But if you win many battles and are a wily, ruthless politician, you might fight your way to be shogun. For centuries, shoguns have been the real rulers of Japan. Most started life as samurai and rose to the top because of their battle skills.

The emperor's role

▼ Since A.D. 794, emperors have lived in the ancient capital city of Kyoto, surrounded by old, noble families. They perform ancient religious rituals and lead quiet lives because they have no political power. Since 1603, the real center of power in Japan has been the shogun's court at Edo, the new capital.

The first shogun

Otomo Yakamochi (died A.D. 786) was the first shogun. He was not a great warrior—just helpful to the emperor.

Shogun for life

Beginning in 1159 two samurai families—the Minamoto and the Taira—fought a terrible war. In 1185 the Minamoto won, and daimyo Minamoto Yoritomo became shogun for life. He was the first shogun to have such power.

Shogun family

▼ The present shogun, Tokugawa Ieyasu is a daimyo from central Japan. He came to power in 1603, and aims to end the fighting. He plans to find daimyo and samurai peacetime jobs as government officials, businessmen, and lawyers. He does not know this, but his family will be shoguns until 1868.

New weapons

▶ A matchlock musket (early European-style gun) made in Japan. Sixteenth-century daimyo, such as Oda Nobynaga, cleverly used the new handheld guns and cannon to defeat their enemies. But when Tokugawa become shogun, he limited the use of all weapons. He did not want daimyo and their samurai armies threatening his power.

A new art form

◀ These tiny objects are netsuke (decorated toggles) used to fasten little pillboxes to a samurai's belt. They are carved in the shape of signs from the Japanese calendar—monkey, boar, and rat—and a cicada, an insect that makes a loud buzzing sound.

Monkey

Cicada

Rat

Boars

Monkeys

What Does the Future Hold?

Don't think of becoming a samurai if you hope for a long, quiet life. Most samurai die young, killed in battle. Life on campaign is hard, and samurai weapons cause terrible injuries. Bushido tells samurai to fight and die rather than to run away or surrender. So, be brave! Aim for a hero's death in battle. It's the best thing a samurai can do. It will bring lasting fame and glory to your family and your lord.

When the fighting's over

▼ If you survive years of fighting, you might retire to a quiet place and become a Buddhist monk. Monks are

Japan's best scholars, famous for their wisdom. Or you might practice calligraphy (beautiful writing). It's a treasured skill— like samurai swordsmanship. It can also be a way of meditating.

Death in battle

▼ If you're killed in battle, an enemy samurai will cut off your head, tie it to his horse's saddle, and carry it back to his daimyo.

Life after death

If you live and die like a good ▶ samurai, people will tell stories about your brave deeds and noble character. These will survive long after you've died. Your life story may even be turned into a play. This woodcut shows a Japanese actor re-creating the adventures of a fierce samurai.

Your future?

▲ When you're old, you may worry about what your next life will be like. Buddhists believe in reincarnation (being reborn). They think your next life will be shaped by your actions in this one. Samurai spend their lives killing—a bad act, according to Buddhists. They say dead samurai will be reborn in new samurai families—a noble, but violent, fate.

Japan's future

If you live after A.D. 1868, don't choose to be a samurai. You'll soon be outdated. Japanese people will still admire old samurai values, such as bravery, but they'll also be looking forward to a new, modern world.

Your Interview

Answer these questions to test your knowledge, then look at page 32 to find out if you have what it takes to get the job.

Q1 What's the best way for a samurai to die?
A bravely in battle
B in a accident
C peacefully at home

Q2 What is the code of behavior that has guided samurai for centuries?
A Buddhism
B *ashigaru*
C Bushido

Q3 Who was Lady Tomoe Gozen?
A a famous Japanese actress
B a legendary female warrior
C the wife of a Japanese emperor

Q4 How do samurai clean their armor?
A by washing it in water
B by scrubbing it with salt
C by hanging it over a smoky fire

Q5 What are the samurai's special weapons?
A spears
B swords
C pistols

Q6 Who is the real ruler of Japan?
A the emperor
B the shogun
C the council of samurai

Q7 What do Noh actors wear to show the character they play?
A masks
B embroidered kimonos
C crests of painted wood

Q8 Which is the highest-ranking samurai?
A *hatamoto*
B daimyo
C *go-kenin*

Q9 What are *kami*?
A reincarnations of Buddhist priests
B Shinto nature spirits
C samurai pillboxes

Q10 How would a daimyo defend his main castle?
A by surrounding it with little forts
B by bribing samurai who are beseiging it
C by building a temple in it

Glossary

Ancestor. Relative who died long ago.

Arquebus. European-style gun, used in Japan in the 16th century A.D.

Ashigaru. Lowest-ranking soldier.

Beseige. To surround with armed forces.

Buddha. Name (meaning "enlightened one") given to Siddhartha Gautama, an Indian prince who lived around 500 B.C.. He taught a new philosophy that showed people how to find peace.

Bushido. Strict rules of brave and honorable behavior followed by samurai.

Campaign. Leading an army to war in enemy territory.

Civil war. A war fought between two groups from the same country.

Daimyo. Top-ranking samurai; land-owning lord.

Genbuku. Ceremony to show a boy has become an adult.

Go. Ancient Japanese board game rather like chess.

Go-kenin. Low-ranking samurai.

Hatamoto. Officers in a samurai army.

Katana. Sword for fighting on horseback.

Kendo. Japanese martial art; players fight each other with bamboo swords.

Kimono. Loose robe with wide sleeves worn by Japanese men and women.

Koku. Unit of measure. Enough rice to feed a man for a year.

Lacquer. Shiny varnish made from the sap of trees.

Meditation. Emptying the mind of everyday thought, to seek truth.

Moat. Deep, wide trench around the walls of a fortified place (such as a castle), usually filled with water.

Ninja. Fighters specially trained as spies and assassins.

Nobori. Banner carried in battle.

Noh. Japanese theatrical drama.

Ramparts. Part of a castle's wall defenses.

Shinto. Ancient Japanese religion based on worshiping nature spirits.

Shogun. Top army commander; shoguns ruled Japan from 1185 until 1868.

Tachi. Long sword for fighting on foot.

Tanto. Dagger.

Toggle. A device for holding or securing.

Tsuba. Decorated sword hilts.

Yari. Spear.

Zen. Branch of Buddhism based on meditation.

Index

Further Reading

Hall, Eleanor J. *Life Among the Samurai*. Greenhaven Press, 1999.
Steele, Philip. *Swords and Samurai: The Ancient Warrior Culture of the East*. Southwater Publishing, 2004.

Have You Got the Job?

Count up your correct answers (*below right*) and find out if you got the job.

Your score:

8 Congratulations! You'll make a good samurai.

7 You're not ready to be a samurai, but we can offer you a job as an ordinary soldier.

5-6 Promising, but you've still got quite a lot to learn.

3-4 Keep on studying, and try again later.

Fewer than 3 Are you sure you want to be a Japanese samurai?

Q10 (A) page 22
Q9 (B) page 14
Q8 (B) page 16
Q7 (A) page 25
Q6 (B) page 10

Q5 (B) pages 3, 26
Q4 (C) page 13
Q3 (B) pages 21
Q2 (C) pages 14, 28
Q1 (A) pages 14, 28